YOU KNOW YOU'RE A CHILD OF THE 1980s WHEN...

Charlie Ellis

summersdale

YOU KNOW YOU'RE A CHILD OF THE 1980s WHEN...

First published in 2004
Second edition published in 2010
This revised and updated edition copyright © Summersdale Publishers Ltd, 2016
Text by Mark Leigh, Mike Lepine and Vicky Edwards

Illustrations by Rita Kovács; icons © Shutterstock

Summersdale Publishers Ltd
46 West Street
Chichester
West Sussex
PO19 1RP
UK

www.summersdale.com

Printed and bound in China

ISBN: 978-1-84953-895-4

Substantial discounts on bulk quantities of Summersdale books are available to corporations, professional associations and other organisations. For details contact Nicky Douglas by telephone: +44 (0) 1243 756902, fax: +44 (0) 1243 786300 or email: nicky@summersdale.com.

To...

From...

YOU KNOW YOU'RE A CHILD OF THE 1980s WHEN...

Amstrad and Commodore still say 'cutting-edge technology' to you.

You drank **Harp** because you believed that it would really stay sharp to the bottom of the glass.

New Romantics aren't the latest page-turners from Mills & Boon.

Opium and **Poison** are substances that hold no fear for you, although death by excessive use of overpowering fragrance is, admittedly, a possibility.

Charles and Diana's Wedding

Widely considered to be the wedding of the century, millions of us tuned in to watch Prince Charles and Lady Diana Spencer get hitched on 29 July 1981. It seemed such a beautiful fairy story back then...

Old-school Telephony

The population of Britain stood at just over 56 million; about half of us had a telephone, and those who didn't used a telephone box, of which there were plenty. Remember being able to make calls for as little as 2p?

NEW TV CHANNELS

Channel 4 began transmission in November 1982. TV with your morning toast followed, with *TV-am* and *Breakfast Time* launching in 1983. Now you could get up early to confirm that there was 'nothing on the telly'.

YOU KNOW YOU'RE A CHILD OF THE 1980s WHEN...

It still amazes you that hairstyles can be achieved with anything less than an entire can of maximum-hold hairspray.

You know that Band Aid is much, much more than a sticking plaster.

You remember when CDs were new and had a certain cachet; they weren't walloped out with every Saturday edition of the *Daily Mail*.

Your 12-year-old crushes were Scott from *Neighbours*, George Michael and the one who is now a bit chubby from Spandau Ballet.

QUIZ

1 What was the name of the toy that gave you words to spell via an electronic voice?

2 What were the names of the pastel-coloured teddies that we all went crazy for?

3 Name the ugly dolls that took their name from a vegetable?

4 Which doll came in tiny pocket sets?

5 What maths aid was Little Professor?

6 Which popular drawing game came onto the market in 1985? (Clue: it's a bit like charades.)

7 Which brand had a schoolhouse as part of its Little People range?

8 A model of which feline-sounding car that featured in a popular TV show was one of the most requested Christmas gifts of the 1980s?

YOU KNOW YOU'RE A CHILD OF THE 1980s WHEN...

You know that The Jam isn't just something to be smeared on your toast but, more importantly, is something to be ever-worshipped in the temple of cool. All hail the Modfather!

**You still want to go to the
High School of Performing Arts
and start paying. In sweat.**

**Packed with peanuts, MARATHON
really satisfies. Whatever Joan
Collins says, it's MARATHON –
not Snickers – you hear?**

**You remember the Queen Vic
opening in *EastEnders*, which
introduced drunken punch-ups,
Dirty Den and Ethel's little Willy.**

Bucket and Spade Package Holidays

These were hugely popular holidays in the 1980s, with the sunniest spots in Europe as the favourite destinations. Free child places were introduced, and having your hols ruined by lairy stag and hen parties was highly unlikely!

Theme Parks

Chessington World of Adventures and Alton Towers followed hot on the heels of the already established Thorpe Park. Boasting American-style roller coasters and other 'big' rides, bumper cars just didn't cut it any more – we discovered our inner adrenalin junkies!

Caravanning

For those who couldn't afford the package holidays, there was caravanning. Modern caravan parks opened up, with more comfort and luxury features. Great for families – even if it meant a fortnight in Wales with rain lashing at the windows.

Birthday Parties

The best birthday parties involved bouncy castles, Wimpy and a VHS copy of *The Goonies*. If you were lucky, your mum might have baked you a cake, but the best thing was having fun with your friends.

Public Swimming Baths

Yes, they still exist, but back in the 1980s they were a hub of social interaction for kids. If you were lucky, you had some kind of slide (possibly inflatable) and giant, raft-like floats to play on. But you'd better stick to the rules printed on those unforgettable signs: no bombing and especially no heavy petting!

Ceefax and Teletext

The internet was yet to emerge, but there was already an on-screen superhighway to surf! You had to press a coloured button to make it appear, and for the most part you did this by accident and wondered how the hell to get *Transformers* back. If nothing else, it was a curiosity.

YOU KNOW YOU'RE A CHILD OF THE 1980s WHEN...

You know that 'The Poison Dwarf' was not one of Snow White's crew.

You still get a craving for
Angel Delight.

Fingerless lace gloves
might make you look like you've
been raiding Great-aunt Maud's
attic but you happen to think
they look cute, quirky and very
'material girl'.

You really wanted
a *Bullseye* 'Bully'.

QUIZ

ONLY A CHILD OF THE 1980s WILL KNOW...

1. What was the name of the ThunderCats' furry, red-and-yellow companion?

2. In the children's art show *Hartbeat*, what were the names of the two main animated clay characters?

3. What was special about Count Duckula's diet?

4. What was He-Man's homeland called?

5 What was the name of Danger Mouse's diminutive sidekick?

6 Who did the Fraggles live in fear of?

7 Who provided voices for the characters in the first series of *Willo the Wisp*?

8 Where did Worzel Gummidge live?

YOU KNOW YOU'RE A CHILD OF THE 1980s WHEN...

It doesn't matter who tries to tell you differently: **Fergie** is not a member of The Black Eyed Peas.

You know **EXACTLY**
who you're gonna call.

You still dream of Club Tropicana
and those free drinks.

If someone talks about 'phoning
home', you immediately want to
do a silly little growly voice and
point your index finger at the sky.

New Romantics

Duran Duran, Talking Heads, The Police, Depeche Mode, Culture Club... all part of the New Wave or New Romantic trend ('post-punk', musically speaking). We all longed to hang out at the Blitz club in London and demonstrate our self-expression and coolness.

Hair Metal

It gave us the likes of Bon Jovi, Van Halen and Aerosmith: rockers with big hair, who made our hearts thump in time to their relentless rhythms; their songs have become some of the most enduringly popular karaoke turns.

HIP-HOP

Hip-hop was new, exciting and brash, brash, BRASH! Run DMC, Beastie Boys, Grandmaster Flash — it was all becoming mainstream and, predictably, our parents loathed it. Which made us even more devoted.

YOU KNOW YOU'RE A CHILD OF THE 1980s WHEN...

You know what they drink in
the jungle and you can still sing
the jingle to prove it.

'Rack off, Bouncer!'
is a phrase that you still use
regularly – with gusto!

You remember when Dennis
Waterman was Arthur's hunky
hired muscle, not a source of
parody on *Little Britain*.

You thought that a gold belcher
chain was a status symbol that
was internationally recognised.
(You were wrong.)

QUIZ

ONLY A CHILD OF
THE 1980s WILL KNOW...

1 Which Michael Jackson song, featuring lyrics about 'Annie', was in the charts in 1988?

2 Which group had a hit with 'You Spin Me Round (like a record)' in 1984?

3 Pepsi and who were a SAW act?

4 What did Mel and Kim say they were 'never gonna be' in 1987?

5 Which girl band 'heard a rumour' in 1987?

6 Who had a hit with 'Never Gonna Give You Up'?

7 Who duetted on 'Especially for You' in 1988?

8 Who had a hit with 'Toy Boy'?

YOU KNOW YOU'RE A CHILD OF THE 1980s WHEN...

The shenanigans of the Gold Blend couple remain one of the most gripping, sexually tense dramas you have ever seen.

Raising Mary Rose means hoisting a 600-ton ship off the sea bed, not waking an elderly lady.

You're still a Numanoid at heart.

You tried to get your nana to go to tap classes so that she could join Les Dawson's Roly Polys.

Pot Noodle

The staple of students, frankly it tasted only marginally better than it smelled. Miraculously, it has endured – what it lacks in nutritional value it makes up for in staying power.

Ice Magic

This sauce, which hardened on ice cream, was the ultimate in pudding paraphernalia. Part-sweet and part-science, the ritual of topping one's sundae and watching it solidify was a truly thrilling experience.

Findus Crispy Pancakes

Minced beef, or chicken, in a kind of unidentifiable sauce – the breadcrumbs and E-numbers were what made it so very moreish and delicious.

Wham Bars

These fizzy, chewy bars of sweet-and-sour goodness were like a fruity explosion in your mouth. And often the cause of that wobbly tooth finally falling out.

Double Dip

Two sherbet flavours were twice the fun! And to make it even better, you could eat the thing you were using to eat the other things. The trick was not to munch too much on your dipping stick otherwise you'd have to tip the remaining sherbet into your mouth (not exactly a bad result).

Cabana Bars

Cabana bars — oozing with caramel, cherry and coconut — were the far more tropical cousin of the humble Bounty bar. Launched in the early 1980s by Rowntree's, Cabana conjured images of golden sands and the bluest of seas while it rotted our teeth.

YOU KNOW YOU'RE A CHILD OF THE 1980s WHEN...

You wanted to do the Gold Run
so badly it hurt...

You still chuckle at the phrase:
'Can I have a "P" please, Bob?'

You'd still like to have a cup of tea and a slice of cake with Worzel, Aunt Sally and the Crowman.

The hole in the ozone layer kept you awake at night and made you think guiltily about the three cans of maximum-hold hairspray you'd used earlier in the day...

QUIZ

1. What did Tim Berners-Lee give the world? (Clue: it's bigger than TV.)

2. In which unforgettable film did Meg Ryan fake an orgasm in a cafe?

3. Which band kicked off a tour called 'Steel Wheels'?

4. What famous barrier was taken down in November 1989?

5 In which square did the Chinese government kill protesting students?

6 What was the name of the boat that collided with a dredger on the River Thames, resulting in 51 deaths?

7 Which topless model and pop singer co-hosted a shambolic Brit Awards?

8 The wreck of which German battleship was located in 1989?

YOU KNOW YOU'RE A CHILD OF THE 1980s WHEN...

When riding the escalator at a London tube station at night, you always glance over your shoulder, just in case a marauding werewolf is on the loose.

You remember thinking that this World Wide Web thingy would never catch on...

You would have happily spent all day playing Pac-Man – if only your mum had let you!

Memories of Birds Eye Steakhouse Grills always make you vocal... Will it be mushrooms? Fried onion rings? We'll have to wait and see. Hope it's chips, it's chips...

Chiffon Scarves

Thanks to artists like Bananarama, Madonna and Cindi Lauper, we were raiding charity shops and our nana's wardrobes for these perfect hair accessories, which ideally needed to be in the brightest possible shades. On reflection, we looked like neon-topped land girls.

Upturned Collars

'Turn it up' was the advice of fashionistas when it came to collars. Jackets or shirts – both, in fact – this was the way a man about town would rock the 1980s look. Even if it did make you look like you had got dressed in the dark.

WORKOUT CLOTHES

Films like *Fame* and *Flashdance* helped to make exercise clothes fashionable. Coupled with the advent of the aerobic craze, leotards, headbands and leg warmers were not just for the gym; there was more Lycra on the streets than could be found in locker rooms.

YOU KNOW YOU'RE A CHILD OF THE 1980s WHEN...

Your party piece is doing the **Rubik's Cube** in less than 40 seconds. That or reciting all the words to '**Vienna**'.

You thought Simon Le Bon
and the other Duran Duran lads
were the finest male specimens
you'd ever seen, even though
they wore lipstick, blusher
and big girls' blouses.

You remember being a bit
suspicious of microwaved
food – you thought it might be
radioactive.

You wore neon socks – odd
ones too – thinking they made
you look 'street'.

QUIZ

1. From which movie does the term 'Bunny Boiler' originate?

2. On which 'street' did a nightmare happen?

3. In which weepy did the song 'Wind Beneath My Wings' feature?

4. What should you not feed after midnight or get wet?

5. Complete the movie title: *Back to the...?*

6 Which Star Wars film was released in June 1983?

7 Who took over the role of James Bond in 1987?

8 Who played Johnny Castle in the film *Dirty Dancing*?

Answers: 1. Fatal Attraction **2.** Elm Street **3.** Beaches **4.** Gremlins **5.** Future **6.** Return of the Jedi **7.** Timothy Dalton **8.** Patrick Swayze

43

YOU KNOW YOU'RE
A CHILD OF THE
1980s
WHEN...

You believed your older brother when he told you that Phil Oakey could only afford half a haircut on his pop star salary.

You did all your school essays on paper with a fountain pen and you would go to the library to do all your research.

You don't remember gap years – people who didn't go straight to uni were just doing resits.

You used to wake up to Mad Lizzie, Rustie Lee, Wincey Willis and Golden Grahams.

Dangly Earrings

Dangly earrings were a big deal. Feathers, beads, diamanté, hoops the size of spaceships... Ears were positively drooping with the weight of big baubles. This was also the decade when having more than one piercing in your ears became fashionable – how much of a load your lobes could bear could have become an Olympic sport.

Sweats

Sweats were sweet. Matching sweatshirt and sweatpants – a reimagining of the 1970s tracksuit – was a combo that every well-dressed bloke had in his wardrobe. Worn with white running shoes, of course.

Shoulder Pads

Made popular by *Dynasty*, this fashion gave us all trouble getting through narrow doorways. And there was always that really annoying issue arising from machine washing, when the pad got rucked up on the spin cycle and you had to spend ages massaging it back into place.

Magnum P. I. Moustache

In the early 1980s a 'Magnum P. I.' moustache was the mark of a man. Decreasing in popularity as the decade rolled by, girls disliked the sensation of kissing what felt like a warm Brillo pad.

Puffball Skirts and Poufy Dresses

These abominable styles of the 1980s meant more flounces than an army of divas deprived of their lipgloss. As they tended to be short, you needed good knees, since this was one thing that the ruff 'n' puff style didn't conceal.

Blousy Jackets

Whether in denim or leather, these were all the go. The fact that you looked eight months pregnant was neither here nor there. George Michael wore one and so did all the Duran boys, ergo you wore one. End of.

YOU KNOW YOU'RE A CHILD OF THE 1980s WHEN...

You were gutted that Prince Charles got married, but decided to hold out for Edward instead.

You graffitied a CND symbol on your school satchel, along with lyrics to The Smiths' 'There is a Light that Never Goes Out'.

You religiously bought every issue of Smash Hits and would test your friends at lunchtimes on the song lyrics printed in the middle pages.

Your Filofax was full of practice signatures for your future life as Mrs Adam Ant.

QUIZ

1. Who played Kevin in *The Wonder Years*?

2. Who was Hilda Ogden's husband in *Corrie*?

3. What was the name of the taxi firm in *EastEnders*?

4. Which soap was set in Summer Bay?

5. Which soap had a chef called Shughie McFee?

6 Which pub did Amos and Mr Wilks pull pints at?

7 Mary the Punk was a character in which soap?

8 Who played sweethearts Scott and Charlene in *Neighbours*?

YOU KNOW YOU'RE A CHILD OF THE 1980s WHEN...

Your pristine Adidas tracksuit, along with a pair of matching shell-toe trainers, still have pride of place in your wardrobe.

You remember Paul McCartney best for being in Wings.

If you didn't have a long shaggy perm, you were a social outcast. Same for your partner.

You used to check your wardrobe for signs of E.T. before going to bed each night – and were always disappointed when there was no sign of him.

Teenage Mutant Ninja Turtles

Found in a sewer and raised by the kindly ninja Hamato Yoshi, Leonardo, Donatello, Raphael and Michelangelo — the 'heroes in a half-shell' — took Turtle Power to the max. Fighting evil, the battle cry of 'Cowabunga, dude!' was heard in playgrounds throughout the decade.

Fireman Sam

Meanwhile, in Pontypandy, Fireman Sam was the 'hero next door' who saved the entire neighbourhood from chip-pan fires, rescued children from disused mineshafts and made sure that we all knew that water and electricity do not mix. Joined by naughty Norman Price and his mum Dilys, cafe owner Bella Lasagne and Station Officer Steele, Elvis Cridlington and firefighter Penny Morris, Sam was always Ready. For. Action!

SHE-RA

Sister show to the ever-popular *He-Man*, *She-Ra* was just as enthralling and entertaining. The set-up was the same, with a group of quirky allies and a legion of baddies, led by the evil Hordak. The magic-sword-swinging and unicorn riding were balanced out by the trademark 'moral' delivered by one of the characters at the end of each episode.

YOU KNOW YOU'RE A CHILD OF THE 1980s WHEN...

You took up keyboard lessons and begged your parents for a walking piano after watching *Big*.

You remember your mates wearing so many crucifixes that you thought there was a massive religious revival.

The four biggest influences on your life were Maggie Thatcher and Stock, Aitken and Waterman.

You once really believed that boys found puffball skirts and pixie boots sexy.

QUIZ

1. Whose famous sketch was about trying to get a 'double seat on a train?'

2. Who advocated that the theme to *The Archers* should be the new National Anthem?

3. Which sketch show featured the 'trucking' song and Gerald the gorilla?

4. Which comic has a sidekick called Fanny the Wonderdog?

5 Which female duo started their TV show in 1987?

6 Which TV funny lady played Mrs Overall in *Acorn Antiques*?

7 'The Ballad of Barry and Freda (Let's Do It)' is a comedy song written by whom?

8 Which Brummie comic had a Saturday night live show called *Carrott's Lib*?

YOU KNOW YOU'RE A CHILD OF THE 1980s WHEN...

You fantasised about going on a date with **The Bangles**.

You learned all you needed to know about self-defence from watching *The Karate Kid*...

... and all you needed to know about sex from *Just Seventeen*.

You asked your careers teacher about opportunities as a Top Gun or a Ghostbuster.

DO YOU REMEMBER...

Dallas

Before all the nonsense of Bobby popping out of the shower and Pammie having dreamt a few series, *Dallas* in its early days was compulsive viewing: full of pouting beauties, alcoholic mothers and evil oil barons. Without the late great Sir Terry Wogan regularly lampooning it on his Radio 2 breakfast show, however, it is arguable whether the show would have won the enviable viewing figures that it did.

Airwolf

Michael Knight's talking car, Kitt, was impressive, but Airwolf could fly and blow the crap out of anything! Plus, the opening theme tune was a rousing synth extravaganza. All in all, this show was guaranteed to give thrills, spills and explosions.

Lovejoy

No question about it. Ian McShane was the hotty of his day. Playing the title role, Lovejoy was the 'bit of rough' antiques dealer who managed to get embroiled in all kinds of crazy capers, very often via snogging posh girls. Still popular today, it is a tribute to McShane that even with that terrible mullet, he is still pretty cute.

Diff'rent Strokes

Child TV stars were nothing new, but they didn't come much cuter or sassier than little Arnold Jackson (Gary Coleman), with his unforgettable catchphrase, 'Whatchu talkin' 'bout, Willis?' The show was family fun, but it also addressed very serious issues like racism and drugs.

Only Fools and Horses

From the minute we met Del Boy and Rodney Trotter we knew that we had found friends for life. Joyous from start to finish, the casting was so spot-on and the writing so good that it seemed like the TV was literally sparkling when we watched. John Sullivan, we salute you.

EastEnders

Kicking off with a nice little murder, the inhabitants of Albert Square first became known to us in 1985, as the Beeb attempted to win a slice of ITV's *Corrie* audience. From Arthur robbing the Christmas Club money, to Little Mo lamping nasty Trevor with an iron, the highs and lows have been funny, heart-warming, terrifying and appallingly acted in equal measure.

YOU KNOW YOU'RE A CHILD OF THE 1980s WHEN...

You remember parties starting with a six-pack of Double Diamond and a bottle of Liebfraumilch, and ending with the contents regurgitated all over your shoes.

You found the woman
dancing in the titles of *Tales of
the Unexpected* erotic
(and you still do).

You wished you could own
something by Sergio Tacchini –
or even just being able to spell it.

You understand what's meant
by a 'seven-inch single'
and a 'C60 cassette'.

QUIZ

Name the product or company from the following advertising slogans.

1. Clean fun. Clean kids. Clean bath.

2. A home's not home without Homewheat!

3. Cup hands, here comes Cadbury's!

4. It's a lot less bovver than a Hover.

5 One instinctively knows when something is right.

6 Tell Sid.

7 We never forget you have a choice.

8 Your two-legged friend.

Answers: 1. Matey bubble bath **2.** McVities Homewheat biscuits **3.** Drinking chocolate **4.** Qualcast Concorde lawnmower **5.** Croft Original Sherry **6.** British Gas **7.** British Caledonian **8.** Wrangler jeans

YOU KNOW YOU'RE A CHILD OF THE 1980s WHEN...

Your dream car at the time was an **XR3i Cabriolet** and your dream job was lead guitarist in **Bon Jovi**.

You wished your dad was Jan-Michael Vincent from *Airwolf*, your mum was Anneka Rice and your girlfriend was Debbie Gibson.

You used to recite entire episodes of *The Young Ones* at the back of the chemistry lab.

Your collection of mint-condition *Transformers* toys is worth far more now than your endowment mortgage.

The Goonies

Is there another film that captures a 1980s childhood so perfectly? Contraptions and gadgets, BMX bikes, water chutes, Cyndi Lauper, older brothers in sweats, pirate adventures, skeletons and a host of weird and wonderful characters. *The Goonies* might just be the all-time greatest kids' movie ever made.

Indiana Jones

You might have been old enough to go to see *Raiders of the Lost Ark* and possibly *The Temple of Doom*. If not, you might have begged your parents to rent *The Last Crusade* on video. In truth, even if you hadn't seen the movies, you knew the name Indiana Jones – and you knew it meant classic swashbuckling action. Though, chances are, you never convinced your parents to buy you a whip.

SHORT CIRCUIT

'Number Five is alive!' Yes, robots were HUGE for 1980s kids. *Transformers* was kicking serious butt in the cartoon arena, but who could deny the appeal of the strangely E.T.-like Johnny 5, brought to life through another staple of 1980s cinema: practical effects.

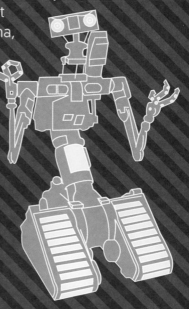

YOU KNOW YOU'RE A CHILD OF THE 1980s WHEN...

The name 'George Michael' makes you think of 'Careless Whisper' rather than careless driving.

Your role models were Gordon Gekko, Donald Trump and Tucker from *Grange Hill*.

'Video nasties' were big news – nowadays, though, they're something you can watch most nights of the week on regular TV.

Your motto then was 'Girls Just Want to Have Fun'. Now you'd just like a bit of peace and quiet while you listen to *The Archers*.

QUIZ

ONLY A CHILD OF THE 1980s WILL KNOW...

1 Which were the two main locations for the Live Aid mega gig? London and...

2 Which band began their The Wall tour in 1980?

3 *Appetite for Destruction* was the name of which band's first tour (and debut album)?

4 Which former Genesis member participated in the 1988 Human Rights Now! tour, for Amnesty International?

5 Which female artist commenced a top-grossing world tour, called The Moment of Truth Tour, in 1987?

6 Which artist went on a Fun Tour to promote her album *She's So Unusual*?

7 The 'Hell's Bell' made its first ever appearance in which hard rock band's tour of 1980–81?

8 Which band opened the Live 8 Wembley show and with which song?

YOU KNOW YOU'RE A CHILD OF THE 1980s WHEN...

You still have your
Pet Monster
in your bedroom.

Partying like it was **1999** once
seemed an eternity away.

**You can remember when drinking
coffee wasn't particularly cool,
and there were only two types to
choose from: black and white.**

**You wanted to marry
Michael J. Fox because,
at the time, he was the
same height as you.**

Guyliner

Guyliner and other 'man slap' can be blamed squarely on the New Romantics, who were very liberal-handed with eyeliner and blusher in particular. Your average disco looked like a casting for a panto.

The Mullet

This legendary yet cringeworthy haircut was really two-in-one: 'business in the front, party in the back'. There was the spiked mullet, the curly mullet and the giant fluffy mullet. They were big, but we admit that they weren't clever. Even if George Clooney, Mel Gibson and Chuck Norris had them, it still doesn't make it right.

THE PERM

Perms were equally as tragic as mullets. It did give you volume – the aim for almost every aspect of women's fashion – but it also kind of made you look as though you'd stuck your fingers in a plug socket. Style icons included Deidre Barlow, Jon Bon Jovi and Whitney Houston. And remember not being able to wash your hair for a week afterwards so that you didn't pull the curl out? Jeez!

YOU KNOW YOU'RE A CHILD OF THE 1980s WHEN...

You used to say, 'By the power of Grayskull, I am He-Man!' – and believed it might work.

Your first personal music player was about four times the size of this book.

The Care Bears and the Smurfs were on your Christmas list (and not because you were being ironic).

Jennifer Beals in *Flashdance* was the most erotic thing you'd ever seen, until you discovered that a man did some of her dancing in the film.

QUIZ

1. Who was the original host of *Blankety Blank*?

2. Who was the original host of *Family Fortunes*?

3. Billed as the 'Euroquiz' and presented by Henry Kelly, what was this TV quiz show called?

4. Who was hosting *Mastermind* in the 1980s?

5 Which show featured Dusty Bin?

6 In which show did Derek Batey ask questions to married couples?

7 Nicky Campbell fronted which game show, starting his stint in 1988?

8 In which game show were contestants urged to 'say what you see'?

YOU KNOW YOU'RE A CHILD OF THE 1980s WHEN...

You would rather go barefoot or stomp around in cereal boxes than wear the trainers your mum bought from British Home Stores.

You remember actually laughing at **Timmy Mallett**, **Hale and Pace, and** **Ben Elton**.

You had more bleach in your jeans and your hair than **Kim Wilde** and **Billy Idol** combined.

You thought that the most knowledgeable authorities on pop music were **Bruno Brookes**, **Jakki Brambles and Peter Powell.**

Sony Walkman

Having arrived at the end of the 1970s, a Sony Walkman was the aspirational gadget of the early 1980s. If only the sponge headphones had not been quite so efficient at stripping blusher off every time you wore it.

Disposable Cameras

The Kodak Fling disposable camera was a huge novelty and made front page news when it launched in 1987. Left on each table for guests to snap each other with, no wedding reception was considered worthwhile unless someone took a pic of the ushers' bums with one of these.

PCs

The first-ever mainstream personal computer, the Macintosh 128K, originally released as the Apple Macintosh, came in a beige case. Coming with a handy handle on the top for easy transport, who needed a laptop?

Casio Calculator

The Casio-80 calculator watch was surely instrumental in giving geeks a crumb of cool? Being able to do times tables and solve equations while telling the time was quite something back in the 1980s.

Answerphones

Domestic answerphones were such fun! Before BT Call Minder we had to record our own message on a specially designed tape recorder that we linked to our landlines — our only lines back then.

Workmate

Initially rejected by Black & Decker, inventor Ron Hickman rubbed his hands in glee when, in 1981, his Workmate caught on and sold its ten millionth unit. TV shows like *Changing Rooms* were still in the future, but Ron spotted an international enthusiasm for DIY and created a gadget that no well-dressed shed could do without.

YOU KNOW YOU'RE A CHILD OF THE 1980s WHEN...

Your make-up bag contained an almost limitless supply of electric-blue eyeshadow and neon lipstick.

Miss World was essential viewing – and fun for all the family!

You once marvelled at the incredible graphics on Thro' the Wall on your **Sinclair ZX Spectrum** – they couldn't possibly get more sophisticated than that, could they?

You can trace your coming of age to the exact moment when the girls in **Bucks Fizz** whipped off their skirts.

QUIZ

1. Which royal baby was born on 21 June 1982?

2. Which Royal married on 23 July 1986?

3. The wedding of Charles, Prince of Wales, and Lady Diana Spencer took place on 29 July 1981. Where did they tie the knot?

4. Which Royal danced with John Travolta at the White House in 1985?

5 A hovercraft named after which royal hit Dover Pier in 1985?

6 Which royal wrote and narrated two films about the Duke of Edinburgh Award for the BBC in 1987?

7 What was the name of the charity sporting event shown on TV in June 1987, featuring members of the royal family?

8 Which royal baby was baptised on 21 December 1984?

YOU KNOW YOU'RE A CHILD OF THE 1980s WHEN...

You remember a time
when movies weren't based
on old TV series.

You bought a Norwegian phrase book on the off-chance that you might bump into Morten Harket when you were down the shops.

You slapped your sister during an argument about who was better looking in CHiPs: Ponch or Jon.

You used Tipp-Ex (and immediately wished you hadn't) to make stripes on your face, just like Adam Ant.

Peugeot 205 GTI

As hot hatches go, the Peugeot 205 GTI was one of the best. One of the most iconic of the decade, it was fast, nippy and stylish. We could hold our heads up in one of these.

Vauxhall Cavalier

The most popular Vauxhall of the 1980s was the Cavalier and over a million of them were sold during the decade. You don't see many about nowadays, though, so maybe they were built for speed rather than longevity. A good 'dad' car.

AUSTIN METRO

Hailed as the 'British car to beat the world', when it rolled off the production line in 1980, the Austin Metro sold well. But it was a swine for rust and, whatever the advertising said, it couldn't beat the damp of a British climate.

YOU KNOW YOU'RE A CHILD OF THE 1980s WHEN...

Your mum let you stay up late just so you could watch the scarier version of the 'Thriller' video.

All the new trends — skinny jeans, Day-Glo colours and giant headphones — give you a distinct feeling of déjà vu.

You didn't care who shot J. R. and you remember wishing someone would murder Roland Rat, but you did have a soft spot for Gordon the Gopher.

You got your first snog at the school disco while slow-dancing to Spandau Ballet's 'True'.

QUIZ

ONLY A CHILD OF THE 1980s WILL KNOW...

1. Which famous John was shot in 1980 by a crazed fan?

2. Which writer, actor and comedian died on 24 July 1980?

3. In which year did Wallis Simpson die?

4. Which Carry On actor died on 15 April 1988?

5. Which Princess and actress died in 1982?

6 Known as the Manassa Mauler, which boxer died in 1983?

7 Half of the singing duo The Carpenters, who lost her battle with anorexia in 1983?

8 Which artist and Surrealist icon died in 1989?

YOU KNOW YOU'RE A CHILD OF THE 1980s WHEN...

You remember buying the first *NOW That's What I Call Music!* album.

You can sing the chorus to 'Physical' by Olivia Newton-John.

You owned a T-shirt that featured Toto's tour dates on the back... or a large smiley face on the front.

You had a mullet to rival those sported by DJ Pat Sharp and singers Paul King and Limahl.

'Gag me with a spoon'

The 'Valley Girl' was one of many regrettable personas to emerge from the sense of entitlement that 1980s culture brought about – more so in the US, but the whiny, annoying slang phrases certainly made it to UK shores eventually, through various movies and sitcoms. 'Gag me with a spoon' indicated your dislike of something (i.e. pass the spoon so I can induce vomiting).

'Fresh'

The rise of hip-hop in 1980s pop culture meant that many of the words and phrases that had been used by the artists themselves for years were all of a sudden opened out to the masses. Rap had a unique vocabulary, which seemed infinitely cool to the legions of young fans. 'Fresh' had nothing to do with sell-by dates – it meant that something was seriously impressive.

'BAD'

Famously, a leather-clad Michael Jackson sung about being 'bad', which is to say 'badass'. This was not a new term, of course, as it had been used for many decades before, but MJ gave it a new lease of life and a funky new twist. Apart from its macho sense, 'bad' was also a way to say that something was 'dangerously good'.

YOU KNOW YOU'RE
A CHILD OF THE
1980s
WHEN...

Your perfume of choice was Poison or Giorgio Beverly Hills, and people knew you were coming 20 paces away.

You remember all the names of Five Star. (OK, they were Stedman, Lorraine, Delroy, Denise and Doris.)

You bitterly recall being made to feel a social pariah because you had a Betamax VCR.

You remember exactly where you were when you heard that Kajagoogoo had split up.

QUIZ

ONLY A CHILD OF THE 1980s WILL KNOW...

1. In which country did the Rubik's Cube originate?

2. Which wristwatch fad included interchangeable straps and faces?

3. Dr Kenneth Cooper was the founder of which 1980s exercise fad?

4. Thanks in no small part to Olivia Newton-John wearing them in the film *Xanadu*, what craze involving specialist footwear was popular in the 1980s?

5 Toru Iwatani created which famous yellow 1980s character?

6 Which toy required balancing and bouncing on a ball at the same time?

7 What kind of bicycle was billed as 'the hottest thing on two wheels'?

8 Which duo was granted the freedom of the City of Nottingham following their incredible sporting achievement of the 1980s?

YOU KNOW YOU'RE A CHILD OF THE 1980s WHEN...

No matter what people say, a part of you still believes that a thin leather tie with a piano keyboard printed on it looks cool.

You remember having to get up off the sofa to change channels – even though you only had four to choose from.

Your idea of sophistication was chicken Kiev accompanied by a glass of Le Piat d'Or.

You were off school for two weeks after dislocating your shoulder while breakdancing.

Daley Thompson

Former decathlete and Englishman Daley Thompson won the decathlon gold medal at the Olympic Games in 1980 and 1984, as well as breaking the world record for the event four times. Which some might say was just showing off.

Ian Botham

Before he started fundraising by going for very long walks, Ian Botham was the finest English cricketer in England and possibly even the world during the 1980s. He was also a bit of a party animal.

Hugo Sánchez

Remember the cartwheeling Mexican footballer? Hugo Sánchez caught the world's attention at the 1986 World Cup by celebrating in athletic style and cartwheeling around the pitch. Bless him.

Fatima Whitbread

This lady meant business! She specialised in the javelin and in 1986 threw 77.44 m, which was a new world record.

Steffi Graf

She had a cool-sounding European name and boy could she play tennis! She achieved a Grand Slam in 1987 and created a huge buzz from commentators and contemporaries alike. Everyone could see she was a star, and she is remembered as one of the all-time greats.

Torvill and Dean

Breathing new life into Ravel's 'Bolero', Torvill and Dean's superb routine took the gold for Team GB in the Sarajevo Winter Olympics with the highest ever scoring routine for figure skaters. And so we all hit the rinks.

YOU KNOW YOU'RE A CHILD OF THE 1980s WHEN...

Your social life used to centre around Trivial Pursuit and Pictionary – or Twister, if your parents were cool.

Even today, you wish that your company Vauxhall Vectra could talk just like Kitt from *Knight Rider*.

Your first introduction to foreign cuisine was a Vesta dehydrated chop suey.

Taking pride of place in your DVD collection are *Footloose, St. Elmo's Fire* and *WarGames*.

QUIZ

Who were the artists or groups who had hits
with the following titles?

1 'Find My Love'

2 'Prince Charming'

3 'Don't You Want Me?'

4 'Kids in America'

5 'Call Me'

6 'Groovy Kind of Love'

7 'Somewhere in my Heart'

8 'Private Dancer'

YOU KNOW YOU'RE A CHILD OF THE 1980s WHEN...

You were sent to your room for dancing on the bonnet of your dad's **Mini Metro** à la *Fame*.

Thanks to *Desperately Seeking Susan*, you still have to fight the urge to dry your armpits with a hand dryer.

You once scored top marks in the *Look-in* 'How Well Do You Know Shakin' Stevens?' quiz.

You were savvy enough to know that Frankie Knuckles was a Chicago house DJ and not an associate of the Krays.

Jackie

Jackie was still the favourite magazine for teen girls, mixing fashion, pop music and agony aunts with a strong subtext that Nice Girls Don't.

Just Seventeen

Or J-17, as it was known, was glossy and sophisticated. A fashion bible for teens, it was the first to really do damage to forerunners like Jackie and quickly outsold its competitors.

SMASH HITS

If you were serious about music then you HAD to subscribe to *Smash Hits*. At the peak of its popularity in the 1980s, the printed lyrics were often learnt in bed at night, when we should have been reading our O-level set books.

YOU KNOW YOU'RE
A CHILD OF THE
1980s
WHEN...

**You believed the hype about
Sigue Sigue Sputnik.**

You aspired to have the muscles of **B. A. Baracus**, but secretly fancied yourself as the new Face.

You still save the **Viennetta** and **Arctic Roll** for your most revered guests.

You secretly still hoped that 2015 would turn out the way it was in *Back to the Future II*.

QUIZ

ONLY A CHILD OF THE 1980s WILL KNOW...

1. What colour did Alice Walker write about?

2. Which Umberto Eco novel was set in Italy in 1327?

3. Who wrote *The Restaurant at the End of the Universe*?

4. Which prolific romantic novelist wrote *Wanderlust*?

5 What kind of verses did Salman Rushdie write?

6 What kind of 'crew' did Stephen King write about?

7 *The Fourth Protocol* was written by which popular eighties author? (Clue: initials 'F. F.')

8 Who wrote *Hollywood Wives*?

YOU KNOW YOU'RE A CHILD OF THE 1980s WHEN...

You often find yourself muttering, 'This time next year, we'll be millionaires!'

You thought your dad was the bee's knees when he pulled out a **brick-sized phone** at your school sports day – your mates were talking about it for weeks afterwards!

You remember that **Captain Birdseye** was half the reason why you ate fish fingers.

You carried your **ghetto blaster** on your shoulder at the park, blasting out **Beastie Boys**.

Thriller

Undeniably the album that defined the decade, and arguably Michael Jackson's finest, if you don't have a copy then you have a gap in your music collection. A big one.

The Hounds of Love

There was something epically fabulous about Kate Bush's fifth studio album and prog rock of a sort. It included the title track, 'Cloudbusting' and 'Running Up That Hill'.

Rio

Duran Duran really took flight with this one, which eventually earned double platinum status for the boys. Not bad for your second album, kids.

Madonna

With her first album just called *Madonna*, it was pretty clear what she was all about (herself). But it remains a classic 1980s album, with 'Lucky Star', 'Holiday' and 'Borderline' all on there.

A Kind of Magic

This was Queen hitting the big time. Reaching number one in the UK, and selling 100,000 copies in its first week, it remained in the UK charts for a whopping 63 weeks.

Brothers in Arms

In 1985 this was Dire Straits at their most prolific: hit after hit after hit. And we played them into the ground. Again and again.

If you're interested in finding out more about our books, find us on Facebook at **Summersdale Publishers** and follow us on Twitter at **@Summersdale**.

www.summersdale.com